STARGAZERS' GUIDES

Could an Asteroid Hit the Earth?

Asteroids, Comets, Meteors, and More

Rosalind Mist

Heinemann Library
Chicago, Illinois

Customer Service 888-454-2279
Visit our website at www.heinemannraintree.com

Design by Richard Parker and Tinstar Design
Illustrations by Jeff Edwards
Printed in China by WKT Company Limited

10 09 08 07 06
10 9 8 7 6 5 4 3 2 1

Library of Congress Cataloging-in-Publication Data
Mist, Rosalind.
  Could an asteroid hit the Earth? : asteroids, comets, meteors, and more / Rosalind Mist.
     p. cm. -- (Stargazers guides)
  Includes bibliographical references and index.
  ISBN 1-4034-7709-4 (lib. bdg.) -- ISBN 1-4034-7716-7 (pbk.)
  1. Asteroids--Juvenile literature. 2. Comets--Juvenile literature. 3. Meteors--Juvenile literature. I. Title. II. Series.
  QB651.M567 2006
  523.44--dc22
                    2005029087

Acknowledgments
The author and publishers are grateful to the following for permission to reproduce copyright material:
Dreamworks p. 31 (Paramount/The Kobal Collection/Industrial Light & Magic); Galaxy Picture Library pp. 6 (Jpl), 11 (NASA), 12 (Robin Scagell), 19 (Robin Scagell), 23 (Stsci), 35 (Robin Scagell), 36 (Juan Carlos Casado), 37, 40 (Uwo/University Of Calgary); Getty pp. 41 (Photodisc), 43 (Photodisc); NASA Goddard Space Flight Center p. 24; NASA Jet Propulsion Laboratory p. 30; Science Photo Library pp. 4 (Jerry Lodriguss), 5 (Roger Harris), 7 (Julian Baum), 8, 15 (Johns Hopkins University Applied Physics Laboratory), 16 (David A. Hardy), 17 (Novosti Press Agency), 18 (Detlev Van Ravenswaay), 21, 26 (Crawford Library/Royal Observatory, Edinburgh), 27 (Royal Greenwich Observatory), 28 (David Jewitt & Jane Luu), 33 (Michael Dunning), 34 (Jonathan Burnett), 38 (Detlev Van Ravenswaay), 39 (Tom Mchugh), 42; Science Photo Library/NASA pp. 13 (Esa/Stsci), 14, 25, 29, 32.

Cover image of an asteroid striking Earth reproduced with permission of the Science Photo Library.

The publishers would like to thank Dr. Geza Gyuk of the Adler Planetarium in Chicago for his assistance in the preparation of this book.

Contents

Words appearing in the text in bold, **like this**, are explained in the Glossary.

Asteroids, Comets, and Meteoroids

We normally think of our **solar system** as the Sun, the **planets**, and their **moons**. However, there are all sorts of other things to be discovered if you know where to look.

Snowballs in space

One of the most impressive things to observe in the night sky is a bright **comet** with a long tail. Comets are like large, dirty snowballs with bits of rock in them. Yet they are much bigger than any snowball on Earth! They can be several miles across—more like icebergs floating through space. Occasionally a comet bright enough to see with the naked eye appears in the sky. However, you need binoculars or a telescope to see most comets.

The great comets are spectacular sights to see.

SCIENCE FACT OR SCIENCE FICTION?

In the film *Armageddon*, there is an asteroid racing toward Earth. Bruce Willis and his team go up in a space shuttle to save Earth. They land on the asteroid and plant bombs on it. When the bombs explode, the asteroid breaks into pieces. This idea might work if an asteroid really were heading for Earth. However, many scientists think that, although the asteroid would break up, the pieces would still hit Earth.

Another type of solar system object is an **asteroid**. Asteroids can be made of rock, metal or carbon, and ice. They are sometimes called planetoids or minor planets. Asteroids can be quite large—up to as much as 600 miles (1,000 kilometers) across. To see an asteroid, you will need a good telescope, since they are usually a long way from Earth.

There are a lot of smaller things out there in the solar system. **Meteoroids** are small chunks knocked off asteroids, planets, moons, or comets. There is also some dust left from the formation of the solar system.

Crash landings

You can see meteoroids as they crash into Earth, creating streaks of light called **meteors** or shooting stars. Some bigger lumps of rock are not completely burned up in the **atmosphere**, and they crash into Earth's surface. They are called **meteorites**.

Meteorites land on Earth every day, but what about comets and asteroids? There is evidence that they have crashed into Earth, the Moon, and other planets in the past, so it is likely to happen again. The question is: when?

Between Mars and Jupiter there is a region called the **asteroid belt**, which contains billions of asteroids of all sizes.

Asteroids or Planets?

Asteroids are found all over the solar system. They **orbit** around the Sun and are made of rock, stone, and ice. They come in all shapes and sizes. Most asteroids are very small, about the size of small boulders. However, there are some much larger asteroids. The largest asteroid in the asteroid belt is called Ceres. It is 580 miles (933 kilometers) across. There are also some large objects beyond the orbit of Neptune. Scientists haven't agreed on the difference between a planet and an asteroid, and asteroids are often also called minor planets.

Asteroids are chunks of rock and metal left over from the formation of the solar system. They come in all sorts of interesting shapes.

HOW IT WORKS:
The long arm of the Sun

The Sun is huge and contains a lot of **matter**. This means that its gravitational pull is very strong and stretches out a long way into space. This gravitational pull keeps the asteroids orbiting the Sun. If an asteroid gets too close to a large planet, the **gravity** from that planet will also tug on the asteroid. This can change the asteroid's orbit and can even make the asteroid crash into the planet.

Orbiting the Sun

Like the planets, asteroids move around the Sun along a path called an orbit. The shape of this orbit is an **ellipse**, which is a crushed circle. Scientists don't just want to know that asteroids are there. They also want to know where they will be next. To do this, they need to figure out the exact orbit of the asteroid. They can use this to predict whether the asteroid will ever hit Earth or another planet or moon. Scientists have figured out the orbits for over 40,000 asteroids so far. The Infrared Space Observatory has estimated that there are between 1.1 million and 1.9 million asteroids larger than 0.6 mile (1 kilometer) in the asteroid belt, so scientists have a lot more work to do.

This is an artist's impression of the asteroid that hit Earth around 65 million years ago, possibly causing the extinction of the dinosaurs.

Where Are Asteroids Found?

Asteroids are divided into four different groups, depending on where they are found in the solar system. These groups are the main belt asteroids, the Trojans, the Centaurs, and the near-Earth asteroids.

The main belt asteroids

The best-known asteroids are the main belt asteroids. These are found in the asteroid belt between Mars and Jupiter. The belt contains about 1.5 million asteroids larger than 0.6 mile (1 kilometers) across, as well as billions of smaller ones. The first asteroids discovered—Ceres, Pallas, Juno, and Vesta—were all main belt asteroids.

The Trojans

Trojan asteroids travel in a similar orbit as Jupiter. Some of them travel around the Sun about a sixth of an orbit ahead of Jupiter, while others follow the same distance behind. Astronomers think that these asteroids have probably been there since the solar system was formed. Since they are moving around the Sun in a similar orbit to Jupiter, they are very unlikely to leave this and hit Earth.

BIOGRAPHY:

Giuseppe Piazzi (1746–1826)

The Swiss astronomer Giuseppe Piazzi was the first person to discover an asteroid. On January 1, 1801, he discovered an object that seemed like a small planet. He named it Ceres, after the Sicilian goddess of grain. It is the largest known asteroid in the main asteroid belt and is 580 miles (933 kilometers) across.

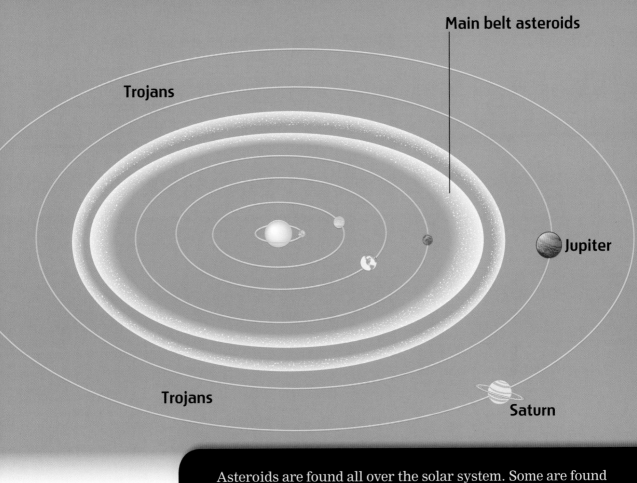

Main belt asteroids

Trojans

Jupiter

Trojans

Saturn

Asteroids are found all over the solar system. Some are found close to Earth and others are beyond the planet Pluto.

The Centaurs

Between the orbits of Jupiter, Saturn, Uranus, and Neptune are the Centaur asteroids. These asteroids don't always stay in the same place. The gravity of the big planets, particularly Jupiter, can pull on them and change their orbits if the asteroids pass too close by. If the asteroids get really close to a planet, gravity can pull the asteroids in and make them orbit the planet. Some of the moons of the giant planets may once have been asteroids.

Near-Earth asteroids

Finally, there are the near-Earth asteroids. These are asteroids dotted around the solar system, and they have orbits that bring them close to the orbit of Earth. Scientists are eager to keep an eye on these asteroids, in case they get too close to Earth and crash into it. Scientists have found over 790 near-Earth asteroids that are more than 0.6 mile (1 kilometer) wide, but there may be many more of them.

What Is an Asteroid Made From?

Not all rocks on Earth are the same—there are many different types. In the same way, asteroids can be made from very different materials. Some asteroids are soft and crumbly, while others are hard and shiny. Some contain metals such as iron and nickel.

Different materials reflect light in different ways. So, scientists examine the way light is reflected from asteroids to find out what they are made from. There seem to be three main types: stony asteroids, metallic asteroids, and carbonaceous asteroids.

Stony asteroids

Stony, or S-type asteroids, make up about 17 percent of all asteroids. These asteroids are bright because they reflect sunlight very well. Eros (see pages 14–15) is an example of a stony asteroid.

Metallic asteroids

Metallic, or M-type asteroids, are made from nickel and iron, just like the **cores** of the planets and moons. Scientists think that these metallic asteroids are probably the remains of planets that did not finish forming. As you might expect, metal can reflect sunlight very well, so these asteroids are also bright. Only about 8 percent of asteroids are metallic. Kleopatra is a metallic asteroid.

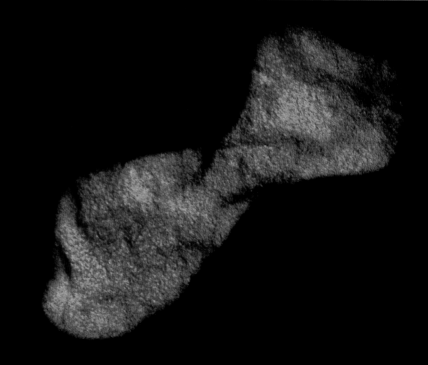

Kleopatra's unusual shape could be due to a collision with another asteroid.

Deimos

Phobos

Some asteroids get caught by a planet's gravity. Scientists think that Mars's moons used to be asteroids.

Carbonaceous asteroids

C-type, or carbonaceous asteroids, are the most common type. Three-quarters of all asteroids are C-type. They are very dark, since they have lots of carbon and tar in them. The two moons of Mars, Phobos and Deimos, are carbonaceous. Scientists think that these were once asteroids, but were then captured by the pull of Mars's gravity.

Shape

Most asteroids are too far away to see clearly, but they seem to come in all sorts of shapes and sizes. Some, like Toutatis, look like knobby potatoes. Others are smoother and more like spheres (balls).

11

Observing Asteroids from Earth

Today, astronomers all over the world are working together to create a catalog of all the asteroids, or minor planets. The Minor Planet Center in Cambridge, Massachusetts, keeps the catalog up-to-date. Details about the asteroids come from all sorts of telescopes, such as the Hubble Space Telescope, huge telescopes in Hawaii, and also small telescopes in people's homes.

Discovering asteroids

New asteroids are being discovered all the time. You could be one of the people who finds one! Lots of asteroids are found by amateur astronomers (people who enjoy astronomy as a hobby). To find a new asteroid, astronomers have to take pictures of the night sky using a telescope that has a camera attached. They take a picture of the same piece of sky at different times. They then compare the images and look for an object that has moved. An asteroid looks like a star, while the planets look like round disks.

To find an asteroid, astronomers compare pictures of the night sky, trying to spot a faint star that has moved.

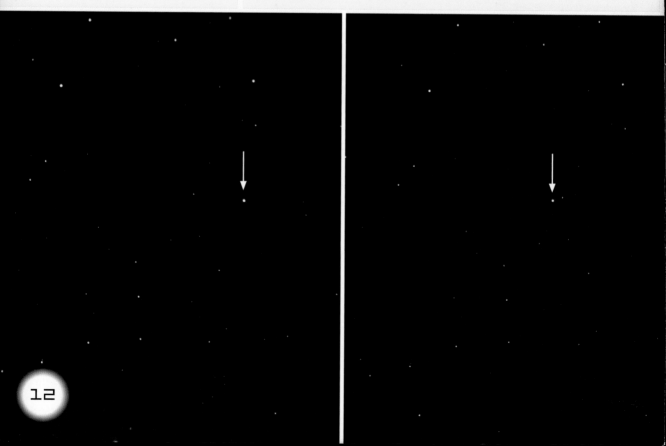

Figuring out the shape of an asteroid

Asteroids are strange shapes and they rotate, sometimes in just a few hours. To us they all look like dots in the sky. Depending on the surface and the shape of the asteroid, it will reflect different amounts of light from the Sun. By measuring this light, astronomers can figure out its shape and how long it takes to rotate.

TRY IT YOURSELF:
See an asteroid

We can see asteroids because they reflect light from the Sun, as planets do. However, they are smaller than planets and far away, so they don't shine very brightly in the sky. The only asteroid that can be seen with the naked eye is Vesta, and even that is very difficult to see. Vesta, Ceres, Pallas, and Juno are the easiest asteroids to look for.

To see an asteroid, you will need a telescope or good pair of binoculars. You will be looking for a "star" that is not normally there, so having a good map of the stars will help. Charts to help you find the minor planets are published in astronomy magazines or on the Internet. Watch the asteroid over several nights and you should be able to see that it has moved against the background of stars.

Visiting Asteroids

The first spacecraft to visit an asteroid was **NASA**'s **space probe** *Galileo* (named in honor of the great Italian scientist Galileo Galilei, 1564–1642). *Galileo* actually passed two asteroids, Gaspra (1991) and Ida (1993). It got really close to Gaspra and discovered that the asteroid is 9 miles (15 kilometers) across. Ida is much larger: it is 35 miles (56 kilometers) long. *Galileo* even found a small moon orbiting around Ida, which was named Dactyl. Scientists have figured out that Ida has lots of holes inside it.

Very few spacecraft have visited asteroids, so this is a very special picture of Ida.

SCIENCE FACT OR SCIENCE FICTION: Mining asteroids

The science fiction writer Isaac Asimov wrote a book called *I, Robot*, which was a series of short stories about robots. In one story, robots mine asteroids for precious metals. Could we really get precious metals from asteroids? Eros, for example, probably contains over 22,000 tons

NEAR-Shoemaker visits Eros

In 2000 another NASA spacecraft, called *NEAR-Shoemaker*, reached the asteroid Eros. Eros is fairly close to Earth (120 million miles, 195 million kilometers). It is an oblong (stretched) shape, 20 miles (33 kilometers) by 8 miles (13 kilometers). *NEAR-Shoemaker* orbited Eros for about a year and took over 160,000 pictures of the asteroid. From these images, scientists identified 100,000 craters and about a million boulders bigger than houses. Then, in February 2001, scientists decided to land *NEAR* on Eros. The spacecraft sent back 69 more images as it landed, but it was damaged during the landing and stopped transmitting.

Bringing asteroid samples back to Earth

Hayabusa is a Japanese spacecraft that is designed to bring back samples of material from an asteroid. This should help scientists find out more about how the solar system was formed. *Hayabusa* was launched in 2003 and is due back to Earth in 2007. The asteroid it will visit is 300 million miles (480 million kilometers) from Earth.

NEAR-Shoemaker was the first spacecraft to land on an asteroid, and it wasn't even designed to do that!

Will an Asteroid Hit Earth?

Asteroids, comets, and meteoroids have hit Earth in the past. So, we can be sure that an asteroid will hit Earth at some point in the future. The big question is: when? Scientists estimate that very large impacts that affect the whole Earth happen about once every 100,000 years. Smaller impacts affecting a country or an ocean happen more often—about once every century.

How close is close?

There are over 3,500 known near-Earth asteroids, about 790 of which are over half a mile wide. These asteroids travel across Earth's orbit. One day, one of these asteroids could crash into us.

Astronomers are watching the near-Earth asteroids and figuring out their exact routes across space. However, with so many asteroids, this takes a long time. It is difficult to figure out the orbit of an asteroid accurately. Astronomers have to make many observations. So far, they haven't discovered an asteroid that is likely to hit Earth.

This is an artist's impression of how the Chicxulub crater was formed. This event may have caused the extinction of the dinosaurs.

SCIENCE FACT OR SCIENCE FICTION: What killed the dinosaurs?

Did an asteroid impact kill off the dinosaurs? A large asteroid impact could cause huge wildfires, **tsunamis**, and volcanic activity. This could reduce the amount of sunlight on Earth for many years. Fewer plants would grow, and animals would have less to eat. So, it is possible that an asteroid impact could have caused the death of the dinosaurs. There is evidence that a large asteroid did hit Earth 65 million years ago (about when the dinosaurs died out). A huge crater has been found that was formed at that time. However, not all scientists agree that this was what caused the dinosaur extinction.

What will happen if we do get hit?

If an asteroid does hit Earth, what will happen? A large object exploded above Tunguska in Russia in 1908. Scientists at the time thought that it was a comet or an asteroid, but they were not sure which. In 2001 Italian scientists reported the results of a long study of the explosion. They think that it was an asteroid that was about 200 feet (60 meters) across, exploding 3 to 5 miles (5 to 8 kilometers) above Earth. It had the same energy as about 1,000 atom bombs. The explosion flattened 830 square miles (2,150 square kilometers) of Siberia. If this had happened over a large city, hundreds of thousands of people would have died.

What Is a Comet?

Every few years, a bright tail of light appears in the skies over Earth. It stays there for days, slowly moving across the sky. If you see something like this, it is probably a comet. The name *comet* comes from the Greek word *kometes*, meaning "long-haired."

A dirty snowball

A comet is sometimes called a dirty snowball or a dirty iceberg. Comets are giant lumps of ice and rock that orbit around the Sun. They spend most of their time in cold regions of space far from the Sun.

In the middle of a comet is the **nucleus**. This is a hard lump of ice and **carbon dioxide ice**, small grains of stone, and dust. The nucleus of a comet is normally about 0.6 to 6 miles (1 to 10 kilometers) long.

This is an artist's idea of what the surface of a comet might look like, with craters and huge lumps of ice.

Melting ice

The nucleus of a comet is too small to be seen from Earth. Yet sometimes a comet's orbit brings it closer to the Sun. When this happens, the outer part of the snowball starts to melt. As the ice warms up, it becomes a cloud of gas surrounding the nucleus. The gas cloud is called a **coma**. It reflects light from the Sun and makes the comet more visible.

Wispy tails

Not all the material that melts stays close to the nucleus. Some stretches away from the nucleus in two very long, wispy tails. These can stretch for millions of miles into space. If the comet is close enough to Earth, the tails can usually be seen without binoculars. One tail is called a dust tail and is made from small particles that are the size of smoke particles. The dust tails look yellow. The second tail is a plasma tail and looks blue. The plasma tail is made of electrically charged gases.

A comet's tail is the biggest thing you can see in the night sky. They can stretch for millions of miles.

TRY IT YOURSELF:

Try making your own comet nucleus. Make a snowball or collect some ice from the freezer and crush it. In a plastic bag, mix the crushed ice with a handful of dirt, a few drops of ketchup, and some fine gravel or sand. Shape the contents into a ball. Put the plastic bag into the freezer and leave it for a couple of hours, until it is really hard. The ice represents the frozen water found on comets and the sand or gravel represents the stony material, as does the dirt, which will make it black. The ketchup represents the carbon-based materials scientists find in comets.

19

Where Do Comets Come From?

Comets were probably formed at the same time as the solar system. There are two kinds of comets: long-period comets and short-period comets.

The Oort cloud comets

Most long-period comets come from a place in the solar system called the Oort cloud. The Oort cloud surrounds the solar system. It is a very long way away, stretching out to about 3 trillion miles (5 trillion kilometers) from the Sun. The comets in the Oort cloud are not just a long way from the Sun. They are also millions of miles away from each other.

How were they made?

When the solar system was forming, most of the material that formed was much closer to the Sun. Scientists think that the Oort cloud comets were formed in the same region as the giant outer planets. The comets gradually got pushed farther away from the Sun by the gravity of the large planets. Eventually they landed up in the Oort cloud. Some may even have left the solar system altogether.

There are many comets waiting to be discovered in the Oort cloud and the Kuiper belt.

Orbits

Kuiper belt

Sun

Oort cloud

The Kuiper belt comets

The second group of comets, the short-period comets, come from the Kuiper belt. The Kuiper belt is much closer to the Sun than the Oort cloud. It is out past the orbit of Neptune, between 2.8 and 4.7 billion miles (4.5 and 7.5 billion kilometers) from the Sun. The Kuiper belt is a disc shape and contains lots of small, icy objects. There may be as many as 35,000 Kuiper belt objects bigger than 62 miles (100 kilometers) across. Not all the Kuiper belt objects are comets, and some scientists think that Pluto and its moon, Charon, are Kuiper belt objects. The first Kuiper belt object was found in 1992 by astronomers using a telescope in Hawaii.

BIOGRAPHY:
Jan Oort (1900–1992)

Jan Oort was born in the Netherlands and worked at the country's Leiden Observatory. He was director of the observatory from 1945 to 1970. In 1950 Oort noticed that comets did not seem to come from outer space. He also found out that comets come from all directions in the sky, and that they have huge orbits. He proposed that they came from a cloud surrounding the solar system. This is now called the Oort cloud.

Jan Oort did not live to see any proof of the existence of the Oort cloud. Even today, astronomers don't have complete proof of its existence.

What Happens to Comets?

Comets travel in a path around the Sun. There are two main kinds of path. Some comets move in periodic orbits. This means that they keep coming back to the same place, just like the planets. Scientists think that other comets move along **parabolic** paths. These comets travel in toward the Sun, swinging around and moving off in a different direction. They will never come back.

The comets moving in periodic orbits can take hundreds or even millions of years to travel once around the Sun. However, some take much less time than this. Encke's Comet, for instance, only takes three and a half years to go around the Sun.

Planets orbit the Sun along paths that are nearly circles. Comets move in orbits much less circular than the orbits of the planets. They are long, stretched ellipses.

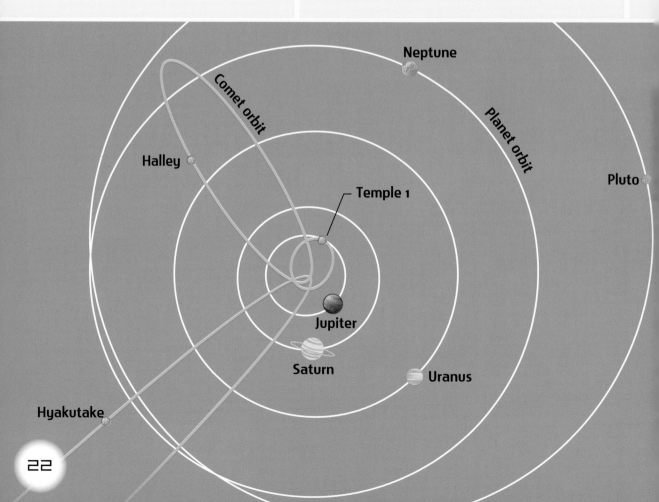

Neptune

Comet orbit

Planet orbit

Pluto

Halley

Temple 1

Jupiter

Saturn

Uranus

Hyakutake

Comet orbits

Sometimes the strong gravity of the large planets changes the orbit of a comet. Halley's Comet came too close to Jupiter on a long-period orbit, or a parabolic path. Jupiter's gravity pulled at the comet and changed it into a shorter periodic comet. Halley's Comet now takes 76 years to orbit the Sun. Gravity can also change a comet's orbit to send it completely out of the solar system.

Disappearing comets

Every time a comet gets close to the Sun, some of its icy nucleus turns to gas and dust. The comet can eventually disappear, leaving just a cloud of dust and gas behind it. Some comets crash into planets or moons. In 1994 Comet Shoemaker-Levy 9 crashed into Jupiter. The crash was spectacular because the comet had split into lots of pieces before it hit Jupiter.

When Comet Shoemaker-Levy crashed into Jupiter, the bigger pieces caused enormous explosions. These left scars in the planet's cloud.

BIOGRAPHY:
Edmond Halley (1656–1742)

Edmond Halley went to Oxford University, in England, but he did not finish his studies. Instead, he did lots of astronomy, mapping the stars in the southern hemisphere.

Halley was the first to realize that comets can travel in orbits. In 1705 he published a book showing that a comet seen in 1682 had the same orbit as comets seen by different people over several hundred years. They were actually seeing the same comet returning again and again. The comet was named Halley's Comet in his honor.

Water on Comets

Comets often contain frozen water and frozen gases of the sort that are now found in the atmospheres of the inner planets. Could there be a connection between comets and the water and gases on planets?

No air or water

When the solar system formed billions of years ago, the planets were extremely hot. Any water or atmospheric gases would have been lost into space. Earth at this time would not have had any air or water.

Shortly after they were formed, the planets were hit by many asteroids and comets. These comets would have contained frozen gases that would have been released on impact. Some scientists think that these gases could have been the source of the atmospheres of the rocky planets (Mercury, Venus, Earth, and Mars). However, other scientists disagree with this theory.

When comets get close to the planets, they can break up into smaller fragments. In 2001 Comet LINEAR broke up in this way. Scientists studying the break-up discovered that LINEAR's water was similar to that on Earth.

University of Hawaii

Hubble Space Telescope
WFPC2

HOT NEWS:

In 2001 scientists in the United States tested the idea that comets could bring life to Earth. They put some of the chemicals needed for life onto a bullet and fired it at high speed into a target. The chemicals survived the collision. Chemicals like these have been found in meteorites and dust clouds in space.

Fragments of comets have been hitting the planets and moons for a long time. They can create chains of craters on the surface, like these on Jupiter's moon Ganymede.

Does water on Earth come from comets?

Comets also contain ice, so they might also have brought water to the surface of the planets. About 1 water **molecule** in 3,200 found on Earth is slightly heavier than normal. This water contains two extra small particles called neutrons. By measuring how many heavy molecules of water there are in different water samples, scientists can tell if the water came from the same place.

Comet LINEAR was studied in 2000, and its water was found to be quite similar to water on Earth. Some scientists think that comets that formed near Jupiter probably had similar water to the water found on Earth. However, evidence from Comet Hale Bopp suggests that Earth's water did not come from comets.

Did comets bring life?

Some scientists suggest that other chemicals needed for life came to Earth on comets. They have already found some signs that these chemicals do exist on comets. To get more evidence, spacecraft will have to visit comets and examine what they are made of. Several spacecraft are already attempting to do this. When they complete their missions, we may find out whether comets really did bring water, and perhaps the other chemicals needed for life, to Earth.

Comets Through History

Comets have amazed and scared people all over the world for many years. Imagine looking up at the sky and seeing a strange streak of light. If you didn't know what it was, you might be worried, too. When they saw a comet or large **meteor shower**, people used to predict that the world would end. This is not so far from the truth. If a large comet did hit Earth, it would cause devastation. However, we now know that most comets we see are too far away to be dangerous.

Comets in different cultures

There are references to fires in the skies in many cultures. They were written about in Babylonia, Persia, China, and in the Bible. In some cultures, people thought that the comet looked like the head of a woman, with long flowing hair. This was seen as a sign of mourning, which meant that the gods were not very happy and something bad would happen. Other people thought that the comet looked like a fiery sword, which meant that a war was coming. Chinese astronomers kept records of the comets they saw for many years. This record-keeping has been very useful to later scientists, who have been able to learn a lot about comet movements from them.

This engraving shows a comet that appeared over Augsburg, Germany, in November 1618. At that time, comets were often regarded as bad omens.

Halley's Comet has appeared every 76 years for over 2,000 years. We are next due to see it in 2062.

TRY IT YOURSELF:
Watch out for a comet

There are 168 named periodic comets, such as Halley's Comet. Depending on their brightness, they can be seen with the naked eye, binoculars, or a telescope. Although comets are always visible from Earth, most are very faint and are hard to see. "Great" comets with long tails, which are easy to see with the naked eye, don't come along very often and are usually unexpected. On average, one appears every five to ten years. It's best to check the Internet to find out when and where comets are visible.

Halley's Comet

The comet that Edmond Halley described in 1705 is one of the most famous comets in history. It can be seen from Earth every 76 years, so plenty of people have had the chance to see it. The earliest record of Halley's Comet is from China in 240 B.C.E., over 2,000 years ago. The comet also appeared just before the Norman Conquest of England in 1066. People thought that the comet was a bad omen (sign) for England's King Harold, and in fact he died in the Battle of Hastings later that year.

Looking at Comets

Very few comets have been visited by spacecraft. This is not surprising, since they are normally so far away. The most visited comet is Halley's Comet. The space probe *Giotto* visited Halley's Comet in 1986, as did four other spacecraft from all over the world. *Giotto* also visited a comet called Grigg-Skjellerup.

Collecting stardust

Stardust is a spacecraft sent by NASA to Comet Wild 2. This comet probably formed near Pluto, right at the edge of the solar system. It has only recently come close enough for us to visit it. The mission reached Comet Wild 2 in January 2004, and *Stardust* flew within149 miles (240 kilometers) of its nucleus. It collected thousands of dust particles from the comet and is due back on Earth in 2006. It will land in the Great Salt Lake desert early in the morning. Scientists are hopeful that the dust will give them new information about the origins of the solar system, or even the origin of life on Earth.

This is a photograph of Comet Shoemaker-Levy 9 orbiting Jupiter. It has split into several pieces. Some of the pieces hit Jupiter in 1994.

HOT NEWS:
A Wild comet

Comet Wild 2 is nothing like scientists expected. The photos from the *Stardust* spacecraft show that there are steep cliffs, tall pinnacles, high, flat areas, and craters on its surface. Scientists were expecting to find that dust left the comet in one jet. However, they found dozens of small regions pushing dust out into space. When *Stardust* flew past the comet, it was hit by bursts of dust, with quiet breaks in between each burst.

Landing on a comet

Rosetta is a spacecraft that was launched by the European Space Agency on March 2, 2004. *Rosetta* is traveling to Comet 67 P/ Churyumov-Gerasimenko. The spacecraft has a very long journey ahead of it—over 480 million miles (800 million kilometers). It will not reach the comet until 2014. When *Rosetta* does arrive, it will orbit the comet. The spacecraft will examine the comet as it comes nearer to the Sun, looking at the way the tail and coma are formed. *Rosetta* will also try to land on the comet. A tiny probe called *Philae* will attach itself to the comet's nucleus.

This is a computer simulation of *Stardust's* sample return capsule arriving back on Earth in 2006.

Deep Impact

Deep Impact is a NASA mission to look inside the middle of a comet. The probe visited Comet Tempel 1 in 2005. Comet Tempel 1 a periodic comet that takes about 5.5 years to orbit the Sun. Its nucleus is estimated to be 9 miles (14 kilometers) long and 3 miles (4.5 kilometers) wide. The comet is visible from Earth using a large telescope. Fortunately, *Deep Impact* got close enough to take some good photos of the comet.

Making a crater on a comet

The *Deep Impact* spacecraft was launched on January 12, 2005, and reached Tempel 1 later that year. The comet was 80 million miles (130 million kilometers) from Earth. As it got close, the main spacecraft released a small impactor spacecraft on a collision course with the comet. On July 4, 2005, the impactor crashed into the comet at 23,000 mph (14,000 km/h), making a hole perhaps 650 feet (200 meters) across. The main *Deep Impact* spacecraft recorded the effects of the collision. Telescopes on Earth and in space also watched as the collision took place.

Deep Impact ready for launch at Cape Canaveral Air Force Station, Florida, in January 2005.

A flash of light

When the impactor hit the comet, there was a large flash of light and clouds of material were thrown off the surface of the comet. Scientists are analyzing the huge amount of data that was gathered during the impact. They hope that their results will give us information about the difference between the inside and the outside of the comet.

SCIENCE FACT OR SCIENCE FICTION?

In the movie *Deep Impact* (1998), a comet is discovered to be heading toward Earth. It is so big that a crash could mean the end of the human race. Politicians must decide what to do to save us. Astronauts are sent to deflect (turn aside) the incoming comet from Earth using nuclear weapons.

Scientists expect a large comet to hit Earth one day, but it probably won't happen for a very long time. They are not sure how we would try to stop it from reaching Earth. If they did decide to explode the comet, the smaller bits would probably still hit Earth. One idea would be to move the comet away from Earth's orbit, but no one is quite sure how we could do that.

Would a comet impact look like this scene from the movie *Deep Impact*?

Meteoroids, Meteorites, and Meteors

Meteoroids are small fragments of rock or metal drifting through space. They come from asteroids, planets, moons, or the dust tail of a comet. Most meteoroids are very small—no bigger than pieces of dust. However, some are much bigger. The biggest meteoroids are 330 feet (100 meters) across. There isn't really a clear difference between asteroids and meteoroids. Some people think of meteoroids as space rocks approaching Earth.

Burning up in the atmosphere

If meteoroids come close enough to Earth, they crash through the atmosphere. When this happens, they burn up. If it is dark, you can see the streaks of light they make in the sky. We call these streaks meteors or shooting stars. If the meteoroid is big enough, it can explode and become something called a fireball. Scientists estimate that millions of meteoroids reach Earth and burn up in the atmosphere every day.

When they enter the atmosphere, meteoroids are traveling very fast. Friction with the atmosphere can make them red-hot.

This is a crater that was made in the window of the space shuttle *Challenger*, possibly caused by the impact of a tiny meteoroid. The picture has been magnified 100 times.

HOW IT WORKS: **High friction**

Why do meteoroids burn up in the atmosphere? The answer is friction. Meteoroids hit the top of the atmosphere at high speed, between 10 and 40 miles (16 and 64 kilometers) per second. The atmosphere is made of different gases, and friction between the meteoroid and these gases slows the meteoroid down. Friction also makes the meteoroid very hot. You can feel how friction heats things up by rubbing your palms together for a minute. At the end of the minute, they will feel very warm.

Crashing to the ground

If a meteoroid is bigger than a marble, it won't completely burn up in the atmosphere. Part of it will crash into the ground. A meteoroid the size of a soccer ball can explode on the way down. Any meteoroid that actually hits Earth is called a meteorite.

Some meteorites fall through the atmosphere at such a speed that the outside gets hot enough to melt. These meteorites have a black crust on the outside. Once it reaches the ground, the crust can start to get rusty and turn orangey-brown. Most of the meteorites we find on the ground are quite small. They are so light that they slowed down quickly and were not melted as they fell through the atmosphere.

Shooting Stars

There is a lot of dust floating around in space. As Earth moves through space, it sweeps up the dust, a little like you would if you walked past a bonfire. The dust particles crash down into Earth's atmosphere. They move so fast that they burn up in the atmosphere and leave a streak of light behind them. The streak of light is called a meteor or shooting star. *Meteor* means "something in the air."

You can look for meteors on any clear night, but you are more likely to see them at certain times of the year. They are best seen with the naked eye rather than a telescope.

Dust in space

Where does all the dust in space come from? As a comet moves through space, it leaves a trail of dust and ice behind it. Meteor showers happen when Earth passes through this trail. Not all meteors come from comets. Some of the dust is left over from the formation of the solar system. There is even a lot of space junk (bits that have fallen off satellites and spacecraft) that can crash into Earth's atmosphere, leaving streaks of light behind them.

TRY IT YOURSELF:
Meteor watching

Random, or sporadic, meteors can be seen every night. They appear on average every ten minutes. In an hour, you could see six meteors. You can't predict what direction they will come from, though. Choose a clear night with a new Moon, since it will be darker and you are more likely to see meteors. It is best to lie down in a place where you can see as much of the sky as possible. Make sure you wear lots of warm clothes, a hat, and some gloves if it is a cold night.

A meteor is a beautiful sight, like a star shooting across the sky.

Fireballs

Fireballs are very bright meteors. They are so bright that if you were outside when one happened, you would see it even if you weren't looking for it. Sometimes fireballs are so bright that they can be seen in the daytime, and occasionally you might even hear an explosion. It is more common to see them at sunset. Most people only see one in their lifetime, but the more you look, the more you are likely to see!

Fireballs are quite rare, but if one happened near to you, you would not be able to miss it!

Meteor Showers

Meteor showers can be spectacular to watch. Instead of seeing five or six meteors an hour, you will see dozens of meteors every hour. You could even see hundreds of them if you are very lucky. In a meteor shower, many streaks of light appear across the sky, like fiery rain. If you leave the shutter on a camera open for a few minutes, you might even capture them on film. Meteor showers happen when Earth passes through a trail of dust left by a comet.

Looking along the path of a comet

If you watch a meteor shower, you might notice that the meteors all appear to come from the same point in the sky. This point is called the **radiant**. The meteor shower is named after the constellation (pattern of stars) where the radiant is. Although the meteors will all seem to go in different directions from this point, they are actually traveling in lines along the path of a comet. They appear to come to a point because of perspective. This is just like looking at long, straight railroad tracks that seem to meet in the distance.

TRY IT YOURSELF:
Catch a meteor shower

The Leonids appear in November. They are at their most spectacular around November 17 and 18. The Perseids are a summer meteor shower. They are best seen around August 12. Some people have been very lucky and witnessed one of the great meteor showers, with dozens of streaks of light crossing the sky,

Artists have often created pictures of meteor showers to record the events.

The Leonids

The most spectacular meteor shower seen in the last century was early in the morning on November 17, 1966. It was a Leonid meteor shower. Over 50 meteors were seen every second. Leonid showers happen every year. The Leonids are caused by Comet Tempel-Tuttle, which was discovered by Ernst Tempel and Horace Tuttle in 1866. Comet Tempel-Tuttle has a 33-year orbit around the Sun, and so Earth passes through a thicker part of the comet's trail about every 33 years. There are lots more meteors when this happens. The earliest recorded sighting of the Leonids was in c.e. 902. The meteoroids travel at about 159,000 miles (257,000 km) per hour. They are very small—about the size of grains of sand.

The Perseids

In 1837 Edward Herrick was the first person to realize that there was a meteor shower every August. He had spotted a now famous meteor shower called the Perseids. They were associated with Comet Swift-Tuttle.

Space Rocks

If a meteor doesn't burn up completely, it will eventually fall to the ground. It is then called a meteorite. Scientists estimate that about 300,000 meteorites fall to the ground every year, although a lot of these fall into the oceans. Most of these meteorites are small: only about 1,000 of them are bigger than a soccer ball. The largest meteorite ever found weighs 66 tons (60 tonnes). It is about 10 feet (3 meters) square and 3 feet (1 meter) high and was found in Hoba, in Namibia.

Falls and finds

Scientists sort meteorites into falls and finds. Falls are meteorites found by someone who saw it land or figured out that one had landed there. A meteorite is called a find if it has been collected by someone who has no idea of when it fell to Earth.

Iron meteorites look so different from normal rocks that you are not likely to mistake them for something from Earth.

Irons

Some meteorites contain iron and are called irons. Most finds are irons because they are so different from normal rocks that they are quite easy to identify. Irons are attracted to magnets, which also makes them easier to find. However, only 5 percent of falls are irons. This shows that this kind of meteorite is quite rare.

Stony meteorites

There are lots of other kinds of meteorites. Chondrites are stony meteorites that have not been melted since they originally formed, soon after the solar system began. Achondrites are stony meteorites that have melted at some point in the past. There are also stony-iron meteorites, which are half stone and half metal. Not all meteorites come from comets or space dust. There are also some lunar (from the Moon) meteorites (currently 31 have been found) and some Martian (from Mars) meteorites (currently 37).

The inside of a meteorite looks quite different than the outside.

Meteorite Hunting

Anyone can find a meteorite. You don't have to be an astronomer or a scientist! Meteorites can fall to the ground anywhere. There could be a meteorite in your garden or a nearby field, on a beach, or in a forest. You need to figure out whether the rocks you pick up are normal rocks or meteorites.

All meteorites will feel heavier than normal rock, but some kinds are easier to spot than others. It is easier to spot metal meteorites, since they aren't like normal rocks. They are mainly made of iron, which is very different from the other rocks you might find.

In Antarctica

The Antarctic is a good place to look for meteorites. This is not because more meteorites fall here, but rather because they are easier to find, since they collect in some areas and are easy to spot against the white ice. The first Antarctic meteorite was found in 1912. A team of scientists visits the Antarctic every year to hunt for meteorites. They find hundreds on each trip.

Meteorites that fall in Antarctica move with the flow of the ice. In places where the ice runs into an obstacle, it is worn away, leaving behind the meteorites.

In the desert

Deserts are another good place to look because they normally don't have many rocks. New meteorites will look black, since they still have the burned crust they developed when coming through the atmosphere. Since they are black, they stand out well against the desert background.

What will we find out?

Meteorites come from all over the solar system. They are very useful because they give us a way to explore space without leaving Earth. Scientists study meteorites to find out about how Earth and the rest of the solar system formed. They also want to know about the different materials that make up the solar system and where they might have come from.

TRY IT YOURSELF:
Find a meteorite

The best place for anyone to look for a meteorite is somewhere meteorites have already been found. You could look in your library to see if anyone has ever found a meteorite near you. Tape a strong magnet to the bottom of a stick (a walking stick or golf club would work well). Push the stick in and out of the undergrowth and near any rocks. Iron meteorites will be attracted to your stick. Remember to get permission from the landowner before hunting for meteorites.

Anyone can search for meteorites—even you!

How Long Before Earth Gets Hit?

Scientists don't know when Earth will next get hit by a large asteroid or comet. They have estimated that roughly every 100,000 years there is a crash large enough to affect the whole Earth. Smaller impacts happen more frequently. Something on the scale of the impact in Tunguska in Russia (see page 17) happens about once every century.

Will it make a big crater?

If Earth does get hit, what would happen? Well, it depends on the size of the object that hits us and where and how it lands. A smaller object that explodes in the atmosphere, like the one at Tunguska, would flatten an area. The impact might also start fires. If an object lands in the ocean, it could create a tsunami. This would damage the coastline around the ocean. If an object reaches land, it would create a crater, like those we see on Mars or the Moon.

A really large object could cause a lot of damage. It could cause an earthquake or activate some volcanoes. A lot of dust and debris would rise into the air and could cover the Sun for a time.

An asteroid could hit Earth anywhere, on land or in the sea.

Watching out for space rocks

Because scientists expect Earth to get hit at some point, they are now getting prepared. There are monitoring stations figuring out the orbits of as many asteroids and comets as possible. By doing this, scientists should be able to provide us with some warning of a crash and maybe even give us a few hundred years to plan what to do. Governments are also starting to think about how they could prevent any collision. It is most likely that they would try to change the comet or asteroid's orbit, so that it would miss Earth completely. They would be unlikely to blow it up, since this would probably mean lots of smaller asteroids hitting Earth instead.

HOW IT WORKS:
The Near Earth Object Program

NASA's Near Earth Object Program is detecting and tracking potentially dangerous objects. It is attempting to locate about 90 percent of the estimated 1,000 large objects (bigger than 0.6 mile, 1 kilometer) that could crash into Earth. About 3,500 near-Earth objects have been discovered so far, and about 790 of these are larger than 0.6 mile (1 kilometer). NASA have classified just over 700 of these as possibly dangerous.

When a volcano erupts, it sends a lot of fine ash high into the air. Some of this ash travels around the world. If enough volcanoes erupted, they could darken the sky across the globe.

How to Watch Meteor Showers

Meteor showers

If you want to watch a meteor shower, choose a dark, clear night and wrap up in warm clothes. Find yourself a patio lounger. Position yourself so you have a good view of the sky, away from streetlamps and as far from buildings as possible.

Meteor shower	When to watch	The peak	Where to watch
Perseids	July 23–August 22	August 12	northern hemisphere
Orionids	October 15–29	October 21	northern and southern hemisphere
Leonids	November 13–20	November 17	northern and southern hemisphere
Geminids	December 6–19	December 14	northern and southern hemisphere

The major asteroids

This table lists the major asteroids.

Asteroid	Mean distance from Sun	Diameter of largest axis	Date discovered	Discoverer
Ceres	257 million miles (414 million km)	597 miles (960 km)	1801	Giuseppe Piazzi
Pallas	258 milllion miles (415 million km)	354 miles (570 km)	1802	Heinrich Olbers
Juno	248 million miles (399 million km)	249 miles (240 km)	1804	Karl Harding
Vesta	219 million miles (353 million km)	329 miles (530 km)	1807	Heinrich Olbers

44

Near-Earth comets

This table shows the comets that will be closer to Earth than one-tenth the average distance between the Sun and Earth between 2006 and 2020. Astronomers do not yet know how bright they will be when they approach Earth.

Comet	Date of closest approach to Earth	Distance from Earth
73P/Schwassmann-Wachmann-C	May 12, 2006	7.1 million miles (11.4 million km)
45P/Honda-Mrkos-Pajdusakova	August 15, 2011	5.6 million miles (9 million km)
P/2004 CB (LINEAR)	May 28, 2014	4.7 million miles (7.5 million km)
P/2000 G1 (LINEAR)	March 22, 2016	3 million miles (4.9 million km)
45P/Honda-Mrkos-Pajdusakova	February 11, 2017	8.1 million miles (13 million km)
46P/Wirtanen	December 16, 2018	7.2 million miles (11.6 million km)

Glossary

asteroid minor planet orbiting the Sun

asteroid belt region between the orbits of Mars and Jupiter that contains many millions of asteroids. It is also known as the main belt.

atmosphere gas held by gravity around a planet or moon

carbon dioxide ice frozen carbon dioxide

coma cloud of gas found around a comet's nucleus

comet large block of ice, rock, and dust that orbits the Sun

core innermost region of a planet or moon, usually made of nickel and iron

crater hole caused by the impact of a comet or meteorite

ellipse regular oval shape

gravity force between all objects that attracts them toward each other

matter "stuff" that everything in the universe is made of

meteor meteoroid that entered Earth's atmosphere and burned up. It is also known as a shooting star.

meteor shower flurry of meteors at a particular time of the year that seem to come from the same point

meteorite meteoroid that entered Earth's atmosphere and reached the surface

meteoroids small fragments of rock or metal that may be pieces of planets, moons, comets, or asteroids

molecule two or more atoms joined together

moon rocky body that orbits a planet

NASA National Aeronautics and Space Administration, the United States space agency

nucleus innermost part of something— for instance, a comet

orbit path of an astronomical object moving around another

parabolic in the shape of a parabola, which is the curved shape of the flight of an object that has been thrown

planet large body of rock or gas that orbits the Sun or another star

radar device used to locate objects that cannot be seen

radiant point in the sky where meteors in a meteor shower appear to come from

radio telescope scientific instrument that can detect radio waves from space

solar system planets and their moons, asteroids, comets, and meteoroids that orbit around the Sun

space probe spacecraft with scientific instruments designed to examine a solar system body

tsunami huge wave generated when a large volume of the sea is displaced suddenly—for instance, after a large undersea earthquake or the impact of a large meteorite

Further Information

Books

Asimov, Isaac, and Richard Hantula. *Comets and Meteors*. Milwaukee: Gareth Stevens, 2005.

Cole, Michael D. *Comets and Asteroids: Ice and Rocks in Space*. Berkeley Heights, N.J.: Enslow, 2003.

Graun, Ken, and Suzanne Maly. *Our Galaxy and the Universe*. Tucson, Ariz.: Ken Press, 2002.

Kerrod, Robin. *The Stars and Galaxies*. Chicago: Raintree, 2002.

Vogt, Gregory. *Asteroids, Comets, and Meteors*. Chicago: Raintree, 2001.

Places to visit

Palomar Observatory
35899 Canfield Road
Palomar Mountain, Calif. 92060-0200
phone: (760) 742-2119

Mount Wilson Observatory
740 Holladay Road
Pasadena, Calif. 91106
phone: (626) 793-3100

Websites

Space and Beyond *http://kids.msfc.nasa.gov/Space/*
A website from NASA about Earth, the Moon, galaxies, and other space stuff. This site also includes the Astronomy Picture of the Day. Every day, this features an incredible picture from space and an explanation of what it is and who took the picture. There is an archive of pictures going back to 1995 and an index organized by subject.

Hubble Gallery *http://hubblesite.org/gallery/*
A gallery of pictures and movies from the Hubble Space Telescope.

Index